Relief Map
poems

Erin M. Bertram

C&R Press
Conscious & Responsible

Summer Tide Pool Chapbook
2016 Second Selection 2 of 3   CB4

All Rights Reserved

Printed in the United States of America

First Edition

Selections of up to two pages may be reproduced without permissions. To reproduce more than four lines of any one portion of this book write to C&R Press publishers John Gosslee and Andrew Sullivan.

Cover Art and Design by Sally Underwood
Interior Design and Layout by Liz Harms

Copyright ©2017 by Erin M. Bertram

ISBN: 978-1-936196-73-9

C&R Press
Conscious & Responsible
www.crpress.org

For special discounted bulk purchases please contact:
C&R Press sales@crpress.org

Thank you for the generous support of our Patreon patrons.

for Marissa

And then they lived happily ever after. *This is not the part of the story that engages us. We want to know what they said, how they looked, what was exchanged between them, what it all meant, and how it all went down. Who was lost, who was found, and why?*

—Stacey D'Erasmo

To have seen such beautiful things. To find oneself placed in their midst. Choiceless.

—Maggie Nelson

CONTENTS

[1] Vulnerability: *to wound*   3

[2] Map: *sheet of the world*   5

Subjunctive Mood   7

[3] Individual: *not divisible, an indivisible thing*   8

[4] Body: *corpse, to be awake, to observe*   11

Kuleshov Effect   13

[5] Quietude: *rest, repose, put back in the same position*   14

[6] Diptych: *pair of writing tablets, folded in two*   16

Documentary Studies   18

[7] Fire: *hot ashes, embers*   19

[8] Bone: *to look at with one eye, to sight*   21

The View from above Deserves to Be Shared   23

[9] Strength: *arrange in a row, fit with a string*   24

[10] Salt: *savory, sweet*   27

Notes   31

Acknowledgments   32

About The Author   33

[1] VULNERABILITY: *to wound*

　　Everything can break, but that doesn't mean it will.

　　Molars, the bones of the face, the forearm, the wrist.

　　The legs, the ground the legs walk on.

　　The knot of pulpy twine we unthinkingly call the heart.

*

　　From the car window, a sky weighted with rain, darkness as when you add a grey wash to a stretch of watered-down blue.

　　That moment before the sky opens up & stays that way.

　　It stays that way.

　　So we touch each other at night, reach through the darkness as if through cloudy water, kneading each other, slowly, like fine-silted clay.

　　Heat-lighting—the sudden startle-blue of it—illuminating our bodies grotesque.

　　Gorgeous.

*

    The plane lifts its heavy body into the air &, from the window, we watch as a field of thistle & prairie grass sways in the distance.

    Or we fill the tank & drive into night's arms, sunflowers along the highway bowing as the wind has its way, though we can't see them, only remember.

    The sound of it—the wind, all this growing & breaking—barely audible.

    Her hand resting on my leg.

    Always the weight of the subjunctive mood.

*

    The body falls, then breaks, every time.

    And, every time, we teach it—foolish, fumbling thing—to get right back up again.

[2] Map: *sheet of the world*

      Consider the body of the beloved—forever uncharted territory, familiar as your own face or hands.

      A map.

      A treasure.

      An X-marks-the-spot in a world vast with unknowns.

      There are places on her body I know the way I know all that's absent of words, a silence so big it demands no extra room, no added floor space or cathedral-ceilinged rooms.

      But we touch & no sparks come, no doves, the earth remains unmoved.

      Simply, we lean into one another & say *yes*.

*

      To carry the expanse of the world in the pocket of your jeans.

      Isn't that what love is, a map to chart the coming days, elevation shaded in, terrain gone over with a fine black pen, tracing contours &

watering holes, valley deep, mountain high, a compass rose in the corner to point the way?

A phrase to roll sweet around the tongue, some sacred words to gather in barrels, show some sign of rain?

*

When she touches my cheek, time bends back upon itself, a bow not yet released.

Heart big as a small wooden boat, I'm a pilgrim lighting out on a strange, forgiving sea.

Come thunder.

Come rain.

Come with me, *dear friend.*

Let me lie beside you watching the clouds until the earth covers us and we are gone.

Subjunctive Mood

Let's touch each other in the forest as the wind tries to push us around.
Let's pretend we're swashbuckling & radiant.
Let's sing into each other's mouths.
Let's eat.
Let's cut our losses & move camp, pitch a tent downriver, tramp through
        the firelight like initiates, & call each other Big Fancy.
Let's climb to high ground & pin our names to the wide back of the sky.
Let's hip & hip.
Let's hooray.
Let's consider all the times we could have broken hearts & did, all the Friday
        nights we spent alone in our pajamas, eating take-out & wishing
        we were beautiful.
Let's spool our indecision around the memory of last night's winnings.
Let's unwind each other by any means necessary.
Let's *thank you thank you* for the mighty spindrift, the hallowed grass stain,
        the peculiar déjà-vu.
Let's drink river water the smart way.
Let's windfall.
Let's birthday cake.
Let's handshake & call it a day.
Let's oscillate wildly when the flashlight goes shy of batteries.
Let's not look down until we dream each other whole, our jeans worn,
        the sun in our eyes, all those miles stacked in our boots.
Let's go.
Let's chaparral & karoo, & urinate beneath only the tallest trees.
Let's press our fears into diamonds, blood dried on our forepaws,
        a little charcoal dusting our cheeks.

[3] INDIVIDUAL: *not divisible, an indivisible thing*

      The body, territory so familiar, sometimes you can no longer make out its rivers & plains, its subtle gradations, vast array of color found in sand & dirt.

      Charting its boundaries lifts us from the lonesome country of the self.

      The shortness of breath.

      The billion nerves rejoicing.

      And when she steals away my heart, I walk slightly bent without it.

*

      The body insists on itself—the fact of its being, of its having been.

      Then the mirror gives back a rounder face, quieter eyes, hands taking shape like your mother's—slender, elegant despite the years of work in them, & all the more sterling for it.

      Breathe in the mallow & sumac & Weymouth pine outside the window, & they, in turn, do the same.

By waking, we wake to the tiny worlds we've made—tacos for dinner, a spearmint-scented bath, a weekend trip west on the interstate for kites & beer brewed in small glass containers.

As for the smallest bones, see the hands, the feet, the inner ear.

*

To discern oneself from the background, retain one's shape in the crowd, solitude the refining agent, the clarity that comes from freezing rain.

To carry a mug of clean water for myself & another to drink from.

The hands almost clean & the favorite shoes set neatly beside the bed.

What it means for one body to trust another—the animal of me, the animal of her—what, at first, appeared to be improbable, then, steadily, less so.

These the grounds on which to map a life?

*

This life as a mown field contained by wilderness.

Yes, it's like that.

It's just like that.

[4] Body: *corpse, to be awake, to observe*

    Evening, the darkness, this time, bore a softness to it.

    She hummed, softly, *when I grow to be a poppy in the graveyard, I will send you all my love upon the breeze.*

    My head on her chest, laying, not lying, not wanting, not wondering, having removed, finally, anxiety's heavy hood.

*

    What spectacular we have spooled up tightly inside us.

    Nightly, the stars revolve above our heads like giant, complex mobiles.

    Like stars.

*

    When she asked, from the passenger seat, what I'd wanted, what warm or shiny thing would suffuse me with joy, I said nothing.

    Instead, the wind moved up & down my body through the open window.

Through the trees—oak, birch, spruce, the multitudinous maples.

An oriole dipped by with its small neon body, nothing but gravel between us & the fields edging the highway.

I told her I wanted her hand between my legs, nestled & still like a sleeping animal.

Like some silent, trusting thing.

Kuleshov Effect

It was as if the hours of first light were an aperture opening out onto a field only we could visit, a field only we knew by its stumblefoot path, & the rest of the day, with its fever & spur, its shadows-in-the-periphery, were slowly closing in around the visible world, making, of the darkness, a kind of inexorable closeness that did not render the light far-flung. Hardly. At noon, the light played the river like a loose drum, only there was no sound—just a little rhythm heard with the eyes. We lifted our shirts to the animals in the sky & placed ice cubes in each other's mouths, stretching words out & out until we made, of silence, a net with which to catch ourselves. Wind, light, water—how it's impossible to distinguish one from the others. A little rain. The scent of pine on our hands. We reach for each other as if there were something inside we were fumbling to work free, with nothing but our bare hands & the memory of having arrived there, intact, no need of a map, no need to tell anyone where we'd gone, or when, if ever, we would return.

[5] Q‍UIETUDE: *rest, repose, put back in the same position*

There is no place where the terrain of the body is not mapped out across the land.

Here, the field spotted with deer.

Here is the bent way we meet each other daily: the photographs, the eye-strain from work, microbrews stocked in the fridge at all times, the hunger—we are stunning in our comfortable brown shoes.

Here is the center of me with a little red flag waving in the wind by a lake, a small lake, for everyone to drink from.

And nobody is ever lonely.

*

August pear, sweet-grain rolled around the tongue, a pocket-knife, grass-stains.

We watch the light change through the open window, color the bed sheets by growing quietly, simply, together, in the dark.

Wear desire like a garment.

Bend to the light between the trees.

Pin our names onto the wide back of the wind.

*

Nights, to draw sleep near, I make, of my hands, a temple—incense, votive, blocks of cool stone, the vocal bow chanting makes of the air.

And deep inside, a soft, low humming in the bones.

A language I know nothing of.

Hush now—it says—*just, hush.*

[6] Diptych: *pair of writing tablets, folded in two*

To hand-rear a life that's unremitting until it stops.

The bowed sun & the sail, the sail & the setting sun.

The compass needle pointing away from home, then gesturing back again.

And the weaving wind, always the weaving wind, both oars broken but still good.

*

Two travelers, salt sailors, sea-drenched pilgrims plotting a shared & separate course, inured to low winds, high pressure, & the slow, swift changing of the tides.

A silent but understood knot between them, frayed lengths of rope taut & thick as a wrist, & an easy familiarity: benchmark, lodestar, signal.

Grocery lists, vibrators, the animal sounds of night pawing our window, prayer flags, the dolphin vertebrae we keep on the bookshelf, all the terrain we have yet to companion our way through.

The crushing number of living things & stars.

*

      To disguise oneself as a better version of oneself, then strip away the ruse & look another squarely in the face.

      To stoke the thinner hours with panels of rough & tumble, a thin veneer, nuzzle the days into nights, nights into days, brilliantly & willfully yoked all the while.

      To light one another from within & stare dumbstruck at the glow.

*

      The body casts shadows.

      On an x-ray, it halts the light in places, others lets it pass through.

      The femur carries most of the body's weight.

Documentary Studies

I.

From a cushioned window seat at 35,000 feet, all attempts at ordering the feral world appear earnest, halfway generous, successful even—latticework of roadways, soft halo of streetlights, green & gold reaches of field, bridges like the backbones of megafauna, the cool geometry of community—the wash of it, through cloudwork, laced with quiet, varnish over daily living things, scene removed just enough—just still enough—to call out in me some sad, sexless desire to press my cheek up against it all.

II.

What makes the Nebraska sky a pool of blue into which you might fall is gratitude—grief, its opposite, its shadow-equal—that somehow, this time, & not without requisite bruises that change color daily, you've made it through. So when you speak—in the grocery line, in the classroom, in bed, under your breath—say *thank you*, *hello*, *my god* like you mean it. The way one horse bows its muzzle into another's stringy mane, nuzzles stubble on lip & chin, up & down, up & down, along the other's broad velvet neck.

III.

Beauty is, at its core, consolation, says the famed essay. And isn't that true, isn't that how we want the story to go. Watch the sky burn off its color. Feel the air drain down. Close your eyes. Take a deep breath. Count to ten. Can't you see, I'm trying to be both present & absent at the same time. Like a blur of flies, photographed, printed on transparencies, layered, one over the other, & the flies disappear.

[7] Fire: *hot ashes, embers*

  Midsummer, late evening, the tent pitched, kindling gathered in half-light stacked in a teepee & lit.

  Cold beer, pine spiking the air with its cool earthen breath, lightning bugs, constellations neither of us could name.

  She taught me how to build a better fire with my hands—how to keep it hungry, how to keep it fed.

  And the flames; the logs whose fuel the flames, slowly, take; & the thinnest rain where the wind might be but was not.

*

  On the thin dirt trail, we walked one-by-one for the width of it, a quiet ache in the joints, the weight carried just another part of the body carrying it.

  We were that at ease with our bodies, dirt lining the fine stitching of our shoes.

*

  What we crave is a circle, drawn deep & in the dirt, within which we will always be safe, or at least not a danger to each other.

Pocket-knives secured but accessible in our packs, matches, the map & compass we needed to make it home.

Fire.

With ease, she laid another branch, thick as a wrist.

And I just stood there, blinking, balancing for words, anything to name the sounds taking shape inside me.

*

When we fell asleep, the tent green & cool against our hands, the crowns of our heads, it was deep.

It was dreamless.

The stars breathing in & out all night.

[8] BONE: *to look at with one eye, to sight*

    Once, I stood in a cathedral made of bone—clavicles, vertebrae, skulls—some partial, some complete.

    The bones of the feet, the hands.

    Eye sockets too big for the eyes.

    Even the pelvis, those most private of bricks.

    The small model skull I took home from that trip lay on the sill below my bathroom mirror until it became too much to look at.

    Until it told me all I needed to know.

*

    A woman, an artist, sits across from strangers in a famous museum, day after day, for three months, eight hours per day—simply, though hardly—holding eye contact with them, not moving, & never once speaking.

    Many museum-goers leave after only minutes, the candor of the stripped-down moment too much to bear in front of a crowd.

Others stick it out, steady their gaze, steady their breath, the minutes opening out before them.

*

To be so fully seen is startling, at first.

And then, still is, only differently.

A ring on both our fingers.

The scaffolding secure.

Every bone exactly where it needs to be.

But connective tissue demands attention, the stretch & ease of the body—of two bodies in close proximity—year after bewildering year.

We, two, moving forward, steadily, fast-bound & bewildered.

The View from above Deserves to be Shared

To impart an intimate knowledge of the land.

The river.

Time & distance.

To study is to consider the sum of an infinite number of small events.

I watch dawn arrive, swirling like vapor along the northeast flank of the mountain.

Warm air wheeling across a brilliant sky.

The river emerging from a dam.

The grinding interface between two, each moving its separate way.

We must begin with the air we breathe.

I'm here on my own, squinting through a juniper at sunset, poppies, snow blowing over a glacier.

Each behaves in its own rhythm.

Nothing could be simpler, nothing more complex.

No other environment varies as rapidly or continuously as the boundary.

The oceans breathing in & out.

[9] STRENGTH: *arrange in a row, fit with a string*

    Winter, dead of: she drove to the Mississippi, parked along the quieter side because she knows the river's filthy waters—its silences—buoy me in ways I can't yet name.

    We got out of the car, went for a walk along the bluff, the austerity of water & ice & wind throwing everything in relief.

    Everything, even the smooth strokes of a hawk, above, cutting the air; our footsteps, boot-heavy, crushing gravel; & a single icicle suggesting itself off the end of a branch, its lone red bud enclosed in a room made entirely of windows.

    We placed our mouths beneath it—remember?—took turns waiting for a single drop to fall, & when it did, were surprised by its salty-sweetness.

    Ice underfoot, the thaw close but entirely hidden, the shortness of breath made visible—tiny clouds of air taking shape before our eyes.

*

    But not winter, not anymore.

    There's a dampness this time of year, a physical reminder of the blooming taking place underfoot, around us, within.

The wild iris, the dandelion, the magnolia & pin oak & birch, & the peonies, their pungent scent of sugar & of sex.

Greenstick spring, its fecund grace, its thrall—heady, pungent, teeming.

A *greening* I once heard it called.

She brings a hand to her lips, applies the honey-flavored balm because her body hasn't yet adjusted to the newfound warmth of spring.

Then she hands the balm to me.

A weed is only a weed because we call it one.

*

When she lived across state lines, I imagined a giant string strung between her chest & mine, fitted, neatly, with a single pin, like a boutonnière to the shirt.

To hold & *to release* in the same broad-arm gesture.

That's one definition of love, isn't it?

To lay very still & to think of nothing—& of her—at the exact same time?

To try to find, in winter, more, despite its discomforts, its tempered darknesses, because it's when she feels most alive?

To wake with the taste of salt & sugar on the tongue, our four arms branches, reaching in the same direction?

[10] Salt: *savory, sweet*

    When I say I get wet for her, I mean holistically.

    The palms, the under-arms.

    Of course, the mouth.

    Sometimes, even, the eyes.

*

    She used to take baths as a way of easing into sleep's deep water, before she moved to a house with a leaking tub, before she moved in with me.

    I imagine her, still, lowering herself into the bath, just the small, bright light over the sink turned on, the tub partially in shadow, partially not, cast in a half-light glow.

    A small space into which she might pass & find her way, slowly, into the world of dreams she will not remember on waking.

    Her breasts a pair of harmless, very beautiful jellyfish bobbing just below the water's surface.

*

You know that moment, in a glass elevator when you watch, dumbfounded, as if in slow-motion, & yet with a logic clean as math, the ceiling of one floor become the floor of the next?

That.

It's with that sense of inevitability, that topsy-turvy ease, that she came into my life.

And on a soft bed / delicate / you would let loose your longing.

All the saltwater our bodies make.

And yet, & yet . . .

There is still so much I do not understand.

NOTES

———

The epigraphs are from Stacey D'Erasmo's *The Art of Intimacy: The Space Between* and Maggie Nelson's *Bluets*.

Portions of this manuscript were adapted from and/or reference the following sources: Wordnik, the New Oxford American Dictionary, Jeanette Winterson's Written on the Body, My Brightest Diamond's "I Have Never Loved Someone," Pierre Teilhard de Chardin's The Divine Milieu, Carl Phillips's "Translation," Susan Sontag's "On Beauty," Marina Abramović's The Artist Is Present, Michael Collier's "Publications" listing on his website, Anne Carson's translation of Sappho's "[I simply want to be dead.]," and Lewis Mackenzie's translation of Kobayashi Issa's "[This dewdrop world,]."

ACKNOWLEDGMENTS

I'm grateful to the editors of the following venues who gave some of this work a previous life, at times in different form:

The Academy of American Poets website; *The Blueshift Journal*; *Copper Nickel*; *Cream City Review*; *Drupe Fruits*; *H_NGM_N*; *Indicia*; *Lambda Literary Review*; *Leveler*; the Midwest Writing Center's *Community Poetry* blog; the chapbook *Windfall* (Lettre Sauvage, 2009), which won the 2009 Lettre Sauvage Poetry Prize; and the micro-chapbook *Close Your Eyes, Look at Me* (Gold Wake Press, 2011).

I'm also grateful to the following committees who've offered additional support for my work:

Page 18 was a finalist for the 2015 *Talking Writing* Hybrid Poetry Prize. Pages 18-28 won the 2016 Gaffney/Academy of American Poets Prize at University of Nebraska-Lincoln. This chapbook was also part of a manuscript that won a 2016 Karen Dunning Scholarly Paper/Creative Activity Award from the Women's & Gender Studies Department at the University of Nebraska-Lincoln.

ABOUT THE AUTHOR

Erin M. Bertram is the author of thirteen chapbooks. A former Fellowship Instructor in English at Augustana College, Bertram has received awards and scholarships from the Academy of American Poets, Prague Summer Program for Writers, and the Hambidge Center for the Creative Arts & Sciences. Their work has appeared in *Leveler*, *So to Speak*, *Uprooted: An Anthology on Gender and Illness*, as a published finalist in the *Diagram* Essay Contest, and elsewhere. An LGBTQ advocate and a graduate of Washington University in St. Louis's MFA program, they are working on a doctorate in Creative Writing at the University of Nebraska-Lincoln.

C&R PRESS CHAPBOOKS

C&R Press hosts two chapbook selection periods from June to September and November to March coupled with a reading in New York City each year. The Winter Soup Bowl and Summer Tide Pool Chapbook Series are open to new and established writers in poetry, fiction, essay and other creative writing.

2016 SUMMER TIDE POOL SELECTIONS

Cuntstruck
by Kate Northrop

Relief Map
by Erin M. Bertram

Love Undefined
by Jonathan Katz

2016 Winter Soup Bowl

Notes from the Negro Side of the Moon
by Earl Braggs

A Hunger Called Music: A Verse History in Black Music
by Meredith Nnoka

OTHER C&R PRESS TITLES

FICTION

Ivy vs. Dogg
by Brian Leung

A History of the Cat In Nine Chapters or Less
by Anis Shivani

While You Were Gone
by Sybil Baker

Spectrum
by Martin Ott

That Man in Our Lives
by Xu Xi

SHORT FICTION

Meditations on the Mother Tongue
by An Tran

The Protester Has Been Released
by Janet Sarbanes

ESSAY AND CREATIVE NONFICTION

Immigration Essays
by Sybil Baker

Je suis l'autre: Essays and Interrogations
by Kristina Marie Darling

Death of Art
by Chris Campanioni

POETRY

Negro Side of the Moon
by Early Braggs

Holdfast
by Christian Anton Gerard

Ex Domestica
by E.G. Cunningham

Collected Lies and Love Poems
by John Reed

Imagine Not Drowning
by Kelli Allen

Les Fauves
by Barbara Crooker

Tall as You are Tall Between Them
by Annie Christain

The Couple Who Fell to Earth
by Michelle Bitting

CHAPBOOKS

Cuntstruck by Kate Northrop
Relief Map by Erin Bertram
A Hunger Called Music: A Verse History in Black Music
by Meredith Nnoka

www.ingramcontent.com/pod-product-compliance
Lightning Source LLC
Chambersburg PA
CBHW032105040426
42449CB00007B/1192